What's inside...

page 4

page 16

page 18

Editor: Karen Brown. Designers: Darren
Model Maker: Susie Johns. Artist: Mary Ha

MEMO BOARD!

1 Sketch an elephant shape onto thick card. Draw a circle for its body, 33cm in diameter. Then draw a circle 19cm in diameter, for the head, about 3cm from the first. Draw in the rest of the body using these circles as a guide.

2 Cut out your elephant. If the cardboard is not very thick, you may need to stick two of the same shaped pieces together.

3 Cut out another piece of card the same shape as the head and ears and a piece for the trunk and bowtie. Stick these on the elephant to make it 3-dimensional.

4 Cover the whole thing with three layers of torn paper, pasted on with diluted PVA glue and leave it to dry.

PVA

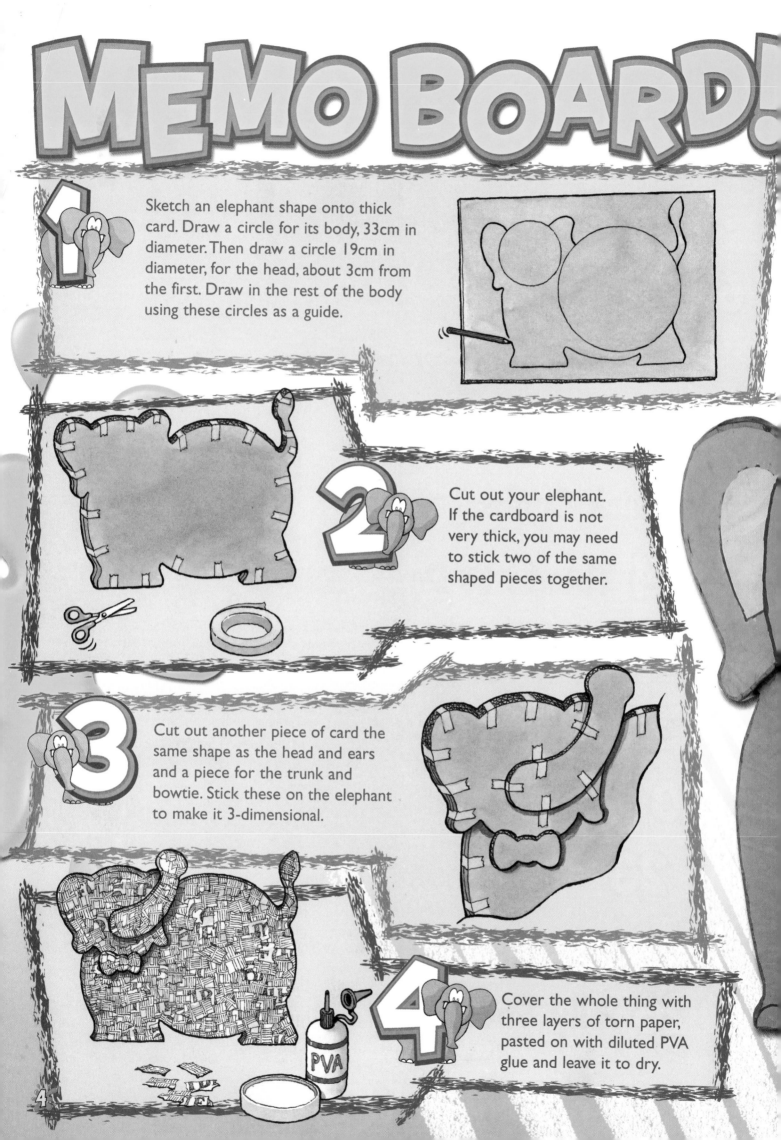

5 Paint it grey with a yellow bowtie and add details in black. Finally paint a circle of blackboard paint on the elephant's tummy. When it's dry go around the edge with yellow. Use chalk to write your memos.

don't forget! mum's birthday

TOMB PAINTER!

GET CREATIVE AND DECORATE SOME ELABORATE ANCIENT EGYPTIAN TOMBS!

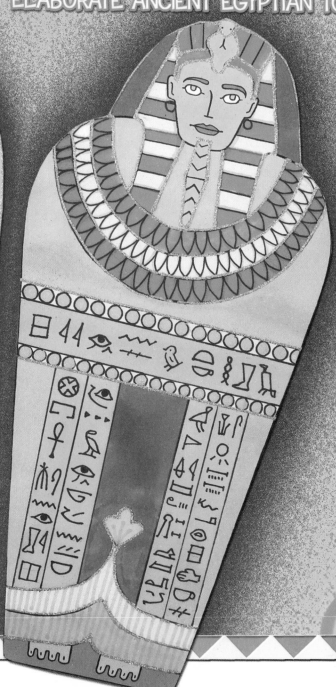

 Trace off or photocopy the Ancient Egyptian coffins from the opposite page onto plain white paper.

 Stick them onto thin card and cut them out.

 Now decorate. You can paint or colour them in and then add detail in black pen. Make them really elaborate by adding glitter or gold or silver paint.

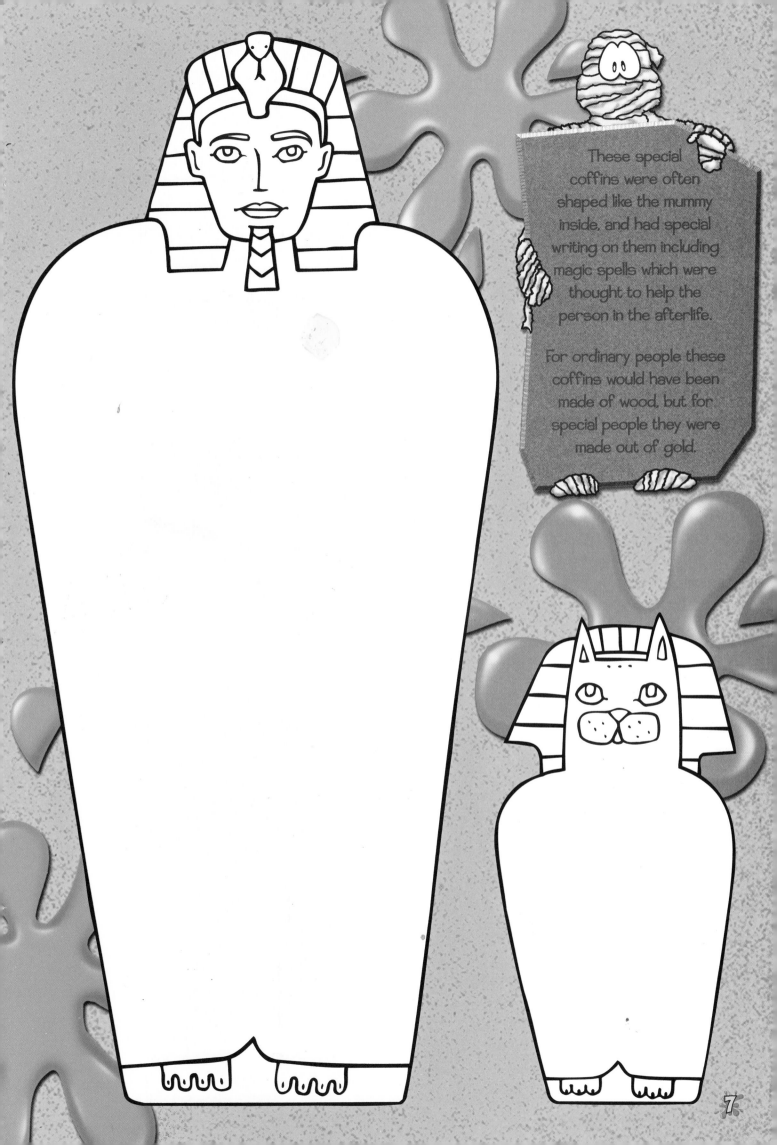

These special coffins were often shaped like the mummy inside, and had special writing on them including magic spells which were thought to help the person in the afterlife.

For ordinary people these coffins would have been made of wood, but for special people they were made out of gold.

7

String Along!

GET MOO-VING AND MAKE THIS GREAT STRING HOLDER!

1

Make the box and lid. (Find a box with a small lid or make a box from cardboard.) You'll need to tape together five pieces of card for each piece. Make the base slightly deeper than the lid.

Hole

2

To help it stay on, make a lip to go inside the lid by sticking strips of card around the inside edge. Then join the lid and the base with a strip of paper, to form a hinge. Make a small hole towards one end of the lid for the string to poke through.

Hole

3

To make the cow, glue a length of cardboard tube to the lid. Cut a notch at one end and add a rolled piece of card for the neck. Add another rolled piece of card for the head. Make a hole over the hole you already made in the tail end.

PVA

4

Pad out the shape of the cow by taping on folded strips of kitchen paper and adding ears cut from card. Leave a small space for the string to be pulled through to form his tail.

YOU WILL NEED:

Cardboard, sticky tape, toilet roll tube, kitchen roll, newspaper, paint, PVA glue, string.

5

Cover the outside of the box and the cow with four layers of papier maché. Make sure you leave the tail hole uncovered. Leave the whole thing to dry until it is rock hard.

PVA

6

Paint the box and the cow using poster paints or acrylics. When the paint is dry, put a ball of string inside the box, pushing one end through the hole.

MONSTER MAD!

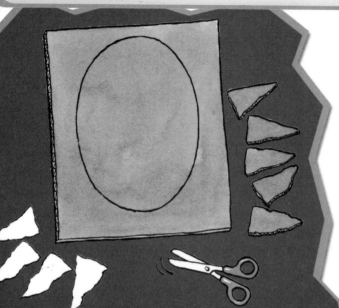

1 Cut out a large oval from a piece of cardboard. Rip some white paper into rough triangle shapes. Do the same with cardboard box card, tearing rough, slightly larger triangles.

2 Glue the cardboard triangles all the way around the card oval, facing inwards. Stick the paper triangles on top of the card ones.

3 When dry, bend the triangles back so it looks like a hole in the wall with torn wallpaper.

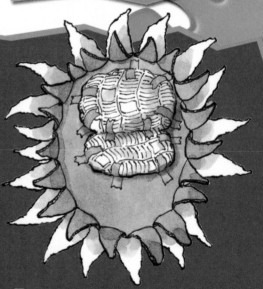

4 To make the top of the head, scrunch up a sheet of newspaper and tape it at the top of the oval. Scrunch up a smaller piece and tape it underneath to make the jaw.

5 Roll up a sheet of newspaper into a thin sausage shape and bend it around to form lips. Use balls of paper for eyes, small sausage shapes for eyebrows and triangles of card for teeth.

6 For the hands, scrunch up two square-shaped balls of newspaper. Roll up some tubes of newspaper and cut them to size for fingers. Tape these to the hands.

7 Attach the hands under the face. Now cover the whole thing with three layers of torn newspaper pasted on with PVA glue. Leave it to dry.

PVA

8 Paint black all the way around your monster to make it look like a hole then paint him green. Paint the mouth red, and eyes and teeth white. When the paint has dried, add details with a black permanent marker.

QUICK CRABS!

THESE CUTE CRABS LOOK BRILLIANT AND ARE EASY TO MAKE!

YOU WILL NEED:

Coloured corrugated card, coloured card, scissors, pipe cleaners, googly eyes.

1 Cut oval shapes from coloured corrugated card. Stick these on plain card in a contrasting colour and cut out again.

2 Cut small rectangles of card, fold in half and use them to stick two ovals together like a hinge.

3 Stick pieces of corrugated card, back to back, and cut out pairs of claws using the claw template. Stick these inside the shell, at either side.

4 Make legs from strips of paper or pipe cleaners. Stick these either side of the shell as well.

5 Close and secure the shell and stick on some googly eyes at the front.

THINGS TO DO WITH...

IF YOU'RE HAVING A PARTY, SAVE A FEW PAPER PLATES SO YOU CAN HAVE SOME PLATE-TASTIC ART ATTACKS!

PLATE MATES

TRANSFORM PAPER PLATES INTO FUNNY CHARACTERS.

For the chicken, cut a curved piece out of a larger plate to make the body. Cut a wavy bit from this section and tape it to a smaller plate to make head feathers. Attach the smaller plate to the larger one with a paper fastener to make a head. Attach some feet and paint it.

For the man, use two paper plates for the head and body. Add card arms and legs with paper fasteners then paint.

FISH DISH

THIS 3D FISH MAKES A WICKED WALL DECORATION.

Cut a slit from the edge of a plate into the centre. Overlap the slit edges and tape down on the underside to form a shallow cone.

Stick on cut out cardboard fins, mouth and a tail. Paint the fish all over and let it dry. You can stick on shiny paper or kitchen foil to make the fish scales. Finally paint on an eye.

PAPER PLATES!

POND LIFE

A PAPER PLATE CAN BECOME THE PERFECT PUPPET.

This one is easy to make! You just fold over about a third of a paper plate. Cut out circular shapes to make pop-up eyes. Add a red paper tongue and some cardboard feet. Finally paint the frog green.

PARTY PLATES

YOU CAN EVEN WEAR A PAPER PLATE ON YOUR HEAD.

Cut a paper plate in half then curl it round to make a cone shape. Staple in place. Paint with bright colours - or use a brightly patterned plate. Add tissue paper streamers or a pom pom to the top. Attach some elastic or string to the bottom to help keep it on your head!

MONSTER MAKE

GIVE SOMEONE A SCARE WITH THIS PETRIFYING PLATE.

Paint a scary face onto a paper plate. Cut strips of cardboard and punch holes at either end and in the centre. Join the card strips with paper fasteners to form a movable ladder. Join the top pieces of card to the plate.

15

GEISHA GIRL!

JAPANESE GEISHAS WEAR TRADITIONAL KIMONOS - OFTEN ELABORATELY DECORATED. HAVE A GO AT DECORATING THEM YOURSELVES.

Make a small screen tidy or greetings card by tracing off both sides onto folded card. Decorate as you wish. Use 3D paints and gold and silver to create a really elaborate gown.

If you cut the geisha girl out you can make a book mark. I looked up some Japanese letters and decorated the sleeves with black felt pen.

SNACK ATTACK!

This loopy lunch box looks great and is fun to make!

1

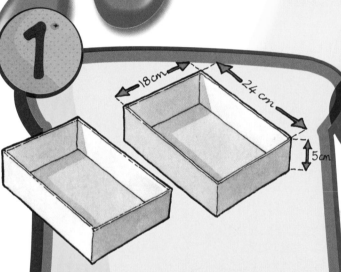

Find a pair of cardboard boxes just the right size. Or simply assemble them from cardboard box card. Start with two boxes measuring about 24cm x 18cm x 5cm.

2

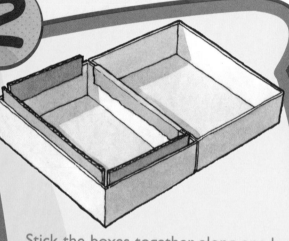

Stick the boxes together along one length using strong tape such as gaffer or carpet tape, to form a hinge. Cut 4cm wide strips of card to fit the length and width of one of the boxes. Stick these inside, half in and half out, to form a lip.

3

Cover the box with three layers of papier maché, avoiding the hinge. Leave it to dry.

4

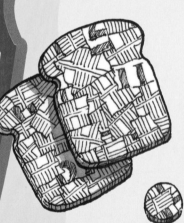

To make the orange, crumple newspaper into a tight ball and bind with sticky tape. For the sandwich, cut sliced bread, cheese and tomato shapes from cardboard. Cover everything with three layers of papier maché.

YOU WILL NEED:
Cardboard, sticky tape,
strong sticky tape,
newspaper, PVA glue, paints.

5

To make a packet
of crisps, start with a
rectangle of card. Tape
folded, crumpled paper to
either side and then cover with
three layers of papier maché and
leave it to dry.

6

Finally paint everything. Paint the
lunchbox and design a lid. Paint the
sandwich, orange and packet of crisps.

ON THE FARM!

MAKE A MINI FARM FROM A CARDBOARD BOX!
IT'S EASY AND HERE'S HOW...

1 Get a large box - cut three sides down to about 8cm high and cut away the fourth side. Cut four pieces of card 6.5cm wide to form stable walls and roofs.

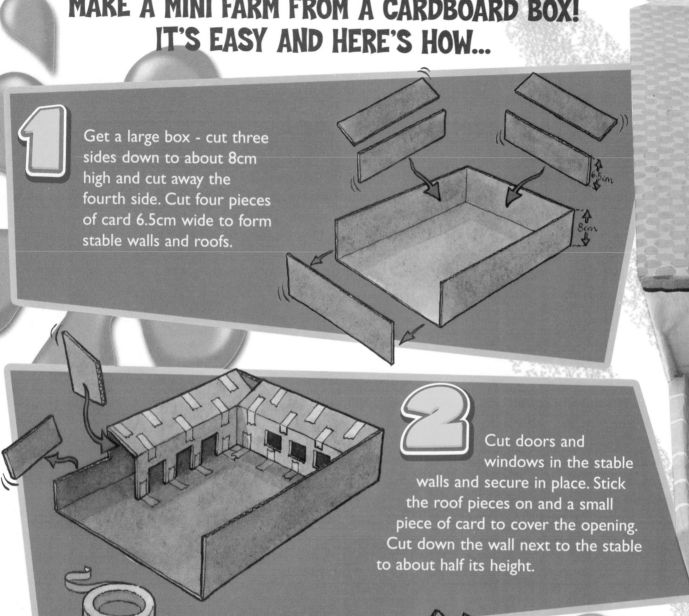

2 Cut doors and windows in the stable walls and secure in place. Stick the roof pieces on and a small piece of card to cover the opening. Cut down the wall next to the stable to about half its height.

3 Make a house out of cardboard. You'll need five pieces - a base and four sides. Use this picture as a guide. Stick it in place against one of the walls.

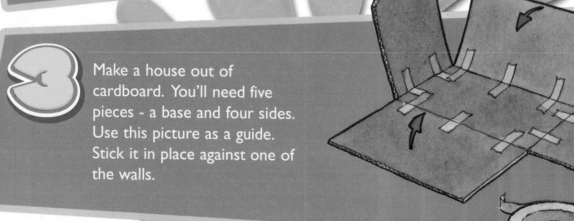

PIPPIN   MOLLY   JESSIE   HENRY

FARM SHOP
EGGS
POTATOES
APPLES
CREAM
CARROTS

CREAM TEAS

4 To make the roof, fold a rectangle in half and tape one side down. Leave the other half open.

Make a porch from four small rectangles of card and stick it to the front of your house.

5 Cover the whole structure with three layers of torn newspaper pasted on with diluted PVA glue. Make sure you papier mâché the roof section separately, to allow it to open and close. Pay attention to the joins. Leave it to dry and then paint it white.

PVA

21

6 Then paint the buildings cream and the roof tops red. Brush a small amount of glue on the base and sprinkle on some sand for a bit of texture. Stick on a pond made from painted card and paint details on the house and stables.

PVA

Place toy animals all around your farm. Write the horse's names on the stables and place a couple inside. When you have finished playing, store the animals inside the farm house.

You could always use tinfoil to make your pond. What about sticking on some scrunched up green tissue to create foliage around the pond?

Paint some little signs and stick them on the farm house wall. What about a shop or a cream tea sign?

Use several different colours of paint to get the brick effect. The walls are yellowy and brown shades while the roofs are shades of red and pink.

FOIL FRAMES!

TRY THIS SIMPLE BUT EFFECTIVE IDEA FOR SMARTENING UP PICTURES AND PHOTOS!

1 Cut a piece of card to any size and shape you want your frame to be.

2 Wrap the frame in aluminium foil and glue in place. Press down firmly to make it as flat as possible.

3 Using acrylics, paint the frame and then leave it to dry.

4 Finally stick your picture or photo to the back of the frame.

COLLECT DIFFERENT COLOURED FOIL FROM SWEETS AND PACKAGING. USE THIS RATHER THAN PAINTING SILVER FOIL.

FAKE FOSSILS!

FOSSILS ARE THE HARDENED, PRESERVED REMAINS OF PREHISTORIC ANIMALS AND PLANTS. CREATE A PIECE OF HISTORY WITH SOME FAKE FOSSILS OF YOUR OWN!

1 Cut simple shapes from thick card (cardboard box card is ideal). If you want to make it even thicker, stick two or more card shapes together.

2 To create a 3D effect, stick on lengths of drinking straw or string using PVA glue.

3 Cover the fossils with two layers of torn newspaper or tissue paper. Use a brush to paste it on with diluted PVA glue. Press the paper into all the nooks and crannies. Leave them to dry.

4 Paint the fossils beige or a sandy colour. While the paint is wet, sprinkle fine sand all over to make it look fossilised.

YOU CAN MAKE FOSSILS OF ALL SORTS OF THINGS - TRY MAKING SHELLS, SMALL CREATURES AND EVEN FLOWERS!

25

SILLY SNOUTS!

THESE ARE FUN FOR A FANCY DRESS PARTY! YOU COULD MAKE A ZEBRA, A PIG, A TIGER OR A LEOPARD, LIKE THE ONES ON THIS PAGE - OR THINK UP SOME IDEAS OF YOUR OWN!

YOU WILL NEED:

Paper cups, elastic or string, paint, scraps of coloured paper, glue stick

You can just paint the snout. Simply paint the paper cup with a single colour, leave it to dry, then add patterns and markings, including nostrils.

Alternatively, you can cover the cup with paper cut outs - like these ripped strips of black paper - just glue them the length of the cup.

Add some whiskers by sticking pipe cleaners into the cup.

Finally, pierce holes on either side of the cup, and thread with a length of elastic, long enough to go around your head.